Practice Tests for Math GOAL 2 Level A—Forms 921M and 922M

Helping Learners Develop Mathematical Thinking Skills, Approach Math with Confidence, and Sharpen their Test-Taking Ability

By

TABLE OF CONTENTS

PREFACE

Dear Instructors,

This book includes four (4) practice tests and is designed to prepare adult learners for the CASAS Math GOALS 2, Level A Forms 921M and 922M. The practice tests align with the CASAS Competencies and meet the rigorous requirements of the College and Career Readiness Standards (CCRS), the National Reporting System (NRS), and the Workforce Innovation and Opportunity Act (WIOA).

Adhering to the CASAS Math GOALS 2 test blueprint, the practice tests assess learners' understanding of the following math areas: *Number Sense and Operations, Consumer Economics, Algebraic Thinking, Geometry, Data Analysis and Statistics, and Pure Mathematics.*

More importantly, this resource increases learners' confidence, guides them to reflect on their learning and progress, and helps them transfer their knowledge to other contexts. Each practice test includes real-world questions that promote deep understanding and practical application of mathematical concepts. An answer key also accompanies each test.

By using this resource, you can save time, distribute practice sessions over several weeks, and assess and reinforce your learners' understanding of math functions and concepts. To order class sets, visit cbledu.com.

The CBL Team,

Your Partner in Student Learning

INTRODUCTION

Dear Math Students,

This resource will help you develop and reinforce your math skills and test-taking ability. It will prepare you for the CASAS Math GOALS 2 Level A test. The practice tests will assess your understanding of the following math areas: *Number Sense and Operations, Consumer Economics, Algebraic Thinking, Geometry, Data Analysis and Statistics, and Pure Mathematics.*

Important Strategies:

Follow the strategies below to develop and reinforce your mathematical thinking skills and test-taking ability.

1. Study and master the four operations (addition, subtraction, multiplication, and division). Learn several strategies to compute and perform operations.
2. Study and master the multiplication table by reviewing it at least once daily (5 to 10 minutes).
3. Look up the meanings of math concepts (e.g., *sum, product, quotient, fraction, triangle*). Try to describe their meanings in your own words.
4. Seek to understand math ideas or the big picture before practicing the details or simple exercises. You can do that by using YouTube videos or Khan Academy.
5. Connect math ideas and concepts to real-world objects or situations. Ask your instructors for real-life examples.
6. Ask clarifying questions to ensure you understand everything before your class ends.
7. Practice solving word problems weekly (20-30 minutes) without distraction (TV, PC, cellphone, noise).
8. Solve math operations and problems on paper. Always show your work—your strategies or reasoning on paper.
9. Study and practice math in a group or with a classmate. Discuss your math solutions and strategies.
10. Explain math ideas and concepts to yourself or someone else orally. After doing this orally, you can also do it using drawings and writing.

11. Always reflect on your progress and strategies. After each practice session or test, identify what works well and why you make certain mistakes. Review and focus on practicing math ideas and concepts you don't understand well.

12. Celebrate your achievements. Any increase in math knowledge is an achievement.

Remember, math skills are essential for success in various aspects of your life, including community involvement, managing family finances, and professional advancement. By committing to completing the practice tests in this book, you'll be setting yourself up for success in your academic pursuits and beyond.

Let's get to work!

HOW TO APPROACH MATH WITH CONFIDENCE

Here are nine (9) practical ways you can overcome math fear and anxiety and build confidence while using this math book:

1. **Start Small:** Begin with easier problems that you can solve to build your confidence before solving harder ones.
2. **Use the book's Strategies:** Take advantage of this resource's strategies and practice tests. They are designed to help you understand, practice, and sharpen your math skills.
3. **Set Small Goals:** Break your math studies into small, achievable goals. Celebrate when you reach these goals to motivate yourself.
4. **Practice Regularly:** Consistent practice makes learning math more manageable. Try to work on math problems a few times a week.
5. **Take Breaks:** If you feel overwhelmed, take a short break. Come back to the math problems with a clear mind.
6. **Ask for Help:** Don't hesitate to seek help when you need it. Ask a teacher or a classmate, or use online resources if you're stuck.
7. **Stay Positive:** Keep a positive attitude about math. Remind yourself that you can handle it and that it's okay to make mistakes as you learn.
8. **Understand, Don't Memorize:** Focus on understanding the math ideas and concepts rather than just memorizing formulas. This understanding will make you feel more confident in solving math problems and taking math tests.
9. **Visualize Success:** Picture yourself successfully solving problems and understanding concepts. This visualization can boost your confidence.

By following these strategies, you will be able to study well and practice math with more confidence.

PRACTICE TEST # 1

You have 50 minutes to answer 33 questions.

1. What is another way to show 1,238?

   A. 1,200 + 200 + 38

   B. 1,000 + 300 + 20 + 8

   C. 1,200 + 3 + 8

   D. 1,000 + 200 + 30 + 8

2. In number 56,718, what digit is in the thousands place?

   A. 6

   B. 5

   C. 7

   D. 8

3. A horse weighs 1,046 pounds. What is the correct way to write this number?

   A. One hundred forty-six

   B. Ten thousand forty-six

   C. One thousand forty-six

   D. One thousand fourteen-six

4. An insect has six legs. How many legs do seven insects have?

   A. 13

   B. 38

   C. 42

   D. 49

5. Amanda plants X flowers equally in eight rows. If she plants nine flowers in each row, what is X?

   A. 17

   B. 72

   C. 81

   D. 78

6. Jacob studied 57 minutes on Wednesday and 82 minutes on Thursday. How much longer did Jacob study on Thursday?

   A. 15

   B. 23

   C. 139

   D. 25

Look at the following receipt:

1015 Marina Drive
San Diego, CA 91945
800-532-1929

Order : 63	03/20/2020
Check : 598	12:18 PM
1 Grill Octopus	$17.99
1 Salmon Tartar	$15.99
1 Oysters - Green NZ	$22.79
2 Grey Goose Lime	$19.38
VISA 4443	Sale
Subtotal:	$76.15
Tax:	$5.33
Total:	$81.48
Transaction Type	Sale
Authorization	Approved
Approval Code	74E4A76
Payment ID	979189D3
Card Reader	Swiped/Chip

7. How many items were purchased?

   A. 4

   B. 5

   C. 7

   D. 3

8. What is the subtotal amount?

   A. $76.15

   B. $81.48

   C. $22.79

   D. $5.33

9. What is the total amount?

   A. $5.33

   B. $19.38

   C. $81.48

   D. $76.15

10. Which item is the most expensive?

    A. Grey Goose Lime

    B. Grill Octopus

    C. Oysters

    D. Salmon Tartar

11. Ten friends share the cost of a restaurant bill. The bill is $100. How much does each person pay?

    A. 90

    B. $11

    C. $12

    D. $10

12. What is B?

$$\mathbf{7(4+6) = \mathit{B} + 42}$$

    A. 11

    B. 28

    C. 24

    D. 32

13. What is the missing number?

$$32 + ? + 19 = 45 + 19 + 32$$

A. 32

B. 45

C. 51

D. 19

14. What is the unknown number?

$$? \times 6 = 54$$

A. 9

B. 48

C. 10

D. 8

15. What is the circumference of a circle with a radius of 1 centimeter? (Use $\pi = 3.14$)

A. 3.14 cm.

B. 1.57 cm.

C. 6.88 cm.

D. 6.28 cm.

16. If the radius of a circle is 10 centimeters, what is the area? (Use $\pi = 3.14$)

A. 628 cm^2

B. 314 cm^2

C. 62.8 cm^2

D. 31.4 cm^2

17. The following shape is a rectangle. What is the perimeter of the rectangle?

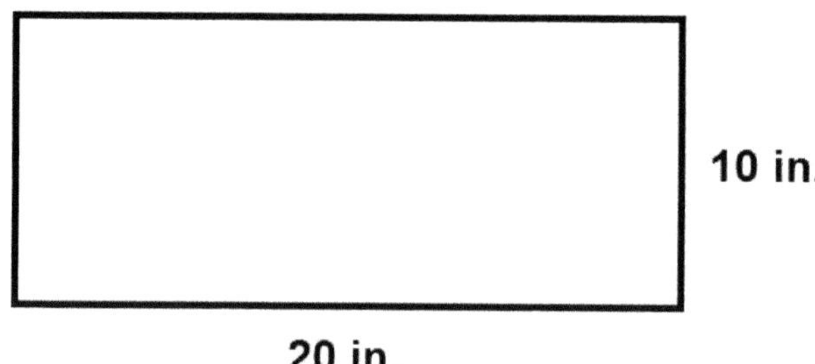

A. 30 in

B. 50 in.

C. 60 in.

D. 45 in.

Look at the following square:

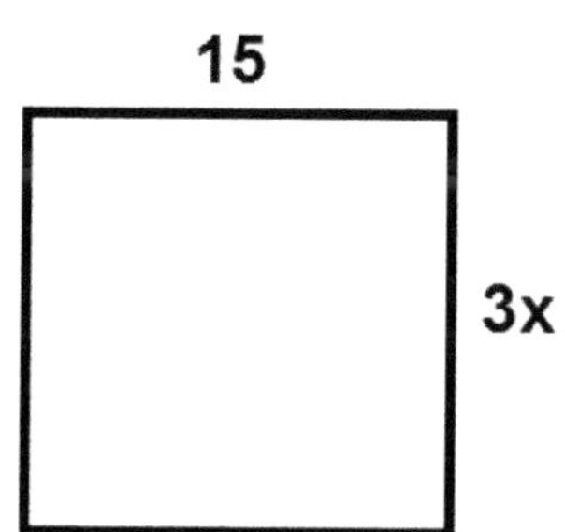

18. What is x?

A. 15

B. 5

C. 3

D. 12

19. What is the perimeter of the square?

A. 60

B. 45

C. 30

D. 18

20. What is the area of the square?

  A. 115

  B. 45

  C. 225

  D. 150

21. What is the missing value?

4.5 kilometers = ? meters

  A. 45

  B. 450

  C. 4,500

  D. 0

Consider the following linear graph:

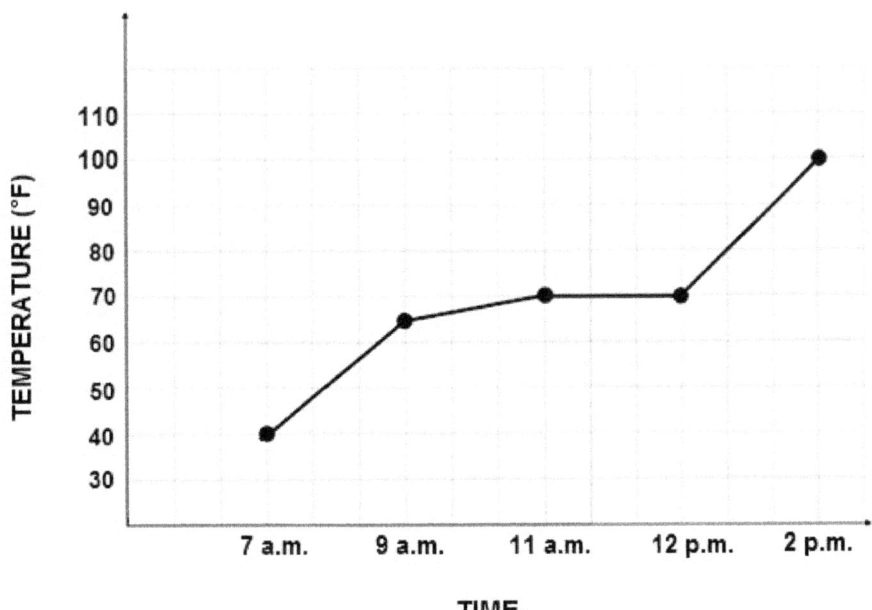

22. What was the maximum recorded temperature?

  A. 70°F

  B. 100°F

  C. 110°F

  D. 90°F

23. What was the minimum recorded temperature?

    A. 30°F

    B. 50°F

    C. 10°F

    D. 40°F

24. At which time of the day was the temperature 100°F?

    A. 12 p.m.

    B. 11 a.m.

    C. 2 p.m.

    D. 9 a.m.

25. What was the temperature at 9 a.m.?

    A. 70° C

    B. 60° C

    C. 65° C

    D. None of the above.

26. According to the linear graph, which of the following is true?

    A. The temperature decreased between 9 a.m. and 11 a.m.

    B. The temperature increased between 11 a.m. and 12 p.m.

    C. The temperature does not change between 11 a.m. and 12 p.m.

    D. The maximum temperature was 90°F.

In a survey about favorite sports, the results were recorded in the following bar graph.

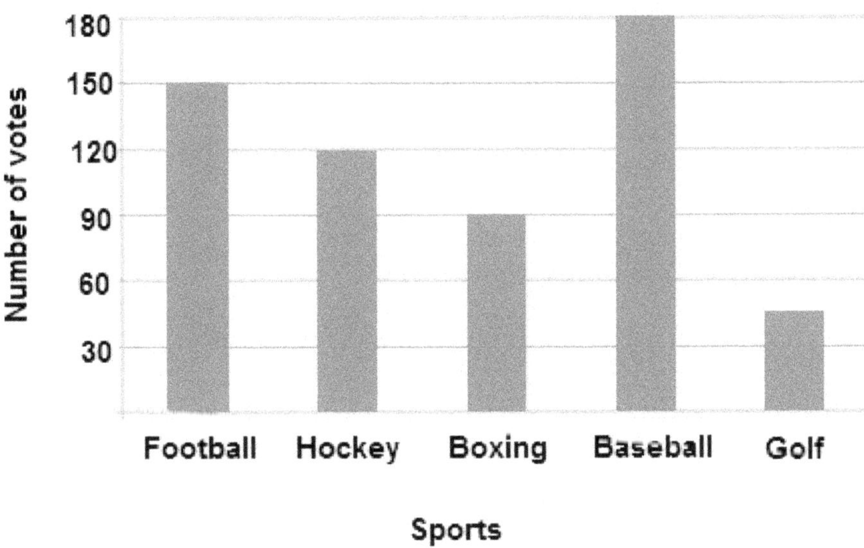

27. Which is the most popular sport?

    A. Football

    B. Hockey

    C. Boxing

    D. Baseball

28. Which is the least popular sport?

    A. Golf

    B. Hockey

    C. Boxing

    D. Football

29. Which sport has 120 votes?

    A. Boxing

    B. Hockey

    C. Football

    D. Golf

30. About how many votes did golf receive?

    A. 60

    B. 30

    C. 50

    D. 45

31. How many fewer votes did boxing receive than hockey?

    A. 30

    B. 20

    C. 60

    D. 40

32. Which of the following is true?

    A. A kilometer is smaller than a meter.

    B. A centimeter is a metric unit of length.

    C. A spoon is a metric unit of volume.

    D. A liter is a non-standard unit of volume.

33. Billy drew four cubes and three squares. How many circular faces did Billy draw?

    A. 7

    B. 4

    C. 2

    D. 0

ANSWER KEY:

1. D
2. A
3. C
4. C
5. B
6. D
7. B
8. A
9. C
10. C
11. D
12. B
13. B
14. A
15. D
16. B
17. C
18. B
19. A
20. C
21. C
22. B
23. D
24. C
25. C
26. C
27. D
28. A
29. B
30. D
31. A
32. B
33. D

REFLECTION ON LEARNING

After completing Practice Test #1, reflect on your performance by answering the questions below. Discuss your responses with your instructor or a classmate.

1. What questions did you answer incorrectly? List the question numbers.

2. Review the list. What types of questions (operations, measurements, algebra, geometry, data analysis, statistics, graph, pie chart) did you answer incorrectly?

3. Review each question you've missed. Why do you think you answered the question incorrectly?

4. Based on the questions you missed, what math functions or concepts do you need to study and practice more? List them.

5. Review the question you got correctly. What strategies or methods did you use? What did you do well?

6. After reviewing all the questions, what questions do you have for your instructor?

PRACTICE TEST # 2

You have 50 minutes to answer 33 questions.

1. Which of the following is equivalent to 8, 000 + 800 + 80 + 1?

   A. 8,818

   B. 8,881

   C. 8,081

   D. 8,188

2. The population of Kansas City is about 509, 295 people. What is this number in word form?

   A. Fifty hundred nine thousand two hundred ninety-five

   B. Five thousand nine two hundred ninety-five

   C. Five hundred nine thousand two hundred nineteen-five

   D. Five hundred nine thousand two hundred ninety-five

3. Sheila walked 75 yards. She needs to walk 39 more yards. How many yards will she walk in all?

   A. 114 yd.

   B. 36 yd.

   C. 116 yd.

   D. 120 yd.

4. Warren studied a total of 49 hours over one week. On average, how many hours did Warren study each day?

   A. 7 hours

   B. 6 hours

   C. 8 hours

   D. 5 hours

5. One dozen donuts costs $6. Darrell bought nine dozen donuts. How much did he spend?

   A. $15

   B. $40

   C. $54

   D. $60

6. What is M + N?

$$6{,}078 = 6{,}000 + M + 70 + N$$

   A. 15

   B. 13

   C. 14

   D. 8

Look at the following table:

Item	Cost
Muffin	$3
Chicken Sandwich	$7
Cheeseburger	$8
Ice Cream	$6

7. What is the total cost of nine cheeseburgers and two ice creams?

   A. $72

   B. $84

   C. $82

   D. $76

8. If Mr. Woods spent $48 on muffins, how many muffins did he buy?

   A. 16

   B. 8

   C. 12

   D. 9

9. Which item is the cheapest?

   A. Cheeseburger

   B. Chicken sandwich

   C. Ice cream

   D. Muffin

10. If Maggie has $100, what is the maximum number of cheeseburgers she can buy?

    A. 13

    B. 10

    C. 12

    D. 8

11. Bob claims that X dimes are $20. What is X?

    A. 20

    B. 100

    C. 150

    D. 200

12. What is X?

    5 dollars + 8 quarters = X cents

    A. 500

    B. 400

    C. 600

    D. 700

13. What is the value of A x B?

    A x 6 x B = 6 x 4 x 7

    A. 6

    B. 11

    C. 28

    D. 7

14. Which expression is equivalent to 8 x 15?

A. 8 x 10 x 5

B. 4 x 4 x 15

C. 4 (2 + 5)

D. 8 (10 + 5)

15. What is the unknown number?

$$? + 34 = 43$$

A. 9

B. 11

C. 77

D. 13

16. An essay contains 28 pages. A revised version includes 17 more pages. What is the total number of pages in the new version?

A. 48

B. 45

C. 11

D. 53

The following figure is formed by a square and a rectangle:

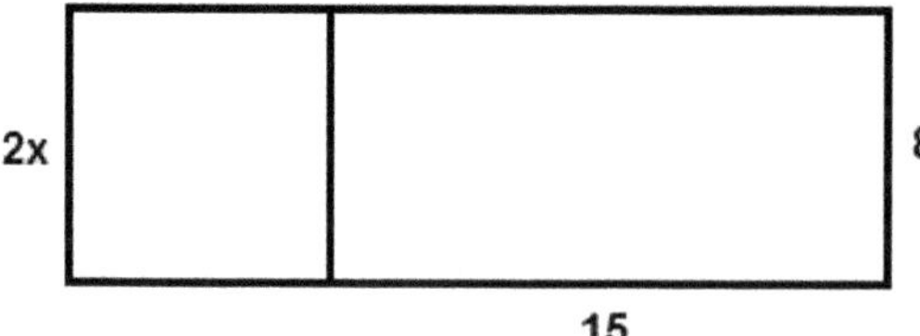

17. What is x?

A. 8

B. 4

C. 6

D. 10

18. What is the perimeter of the square?

    A. 16

    B. 42

    C. 32

    D. 64

19. What is the area of the square?

    A. 64

    B. 32

    C. 46

    D. 120

20. What is the perimeter of the figure?

    A. 46

    B. 54

    C. 58

    D. 62

21. Which unit is most appropriate for describing the weight of an apple?

    A. Grams

    B. Liters

    C. Gallons

    D. Kilograms

22. Which of the following is true?

    A. Millimeter is a non-standard unit of capacity.

    B. Brick is a non-standard unit of weight.

    C. Gallon is a metric unit of weight.

    D. Five meters is greater than five kilometers.

23. How many days are there in ten weeks?

    A. 21 days

    B. 49 days

    C. 17 days

    D. 70 days

24. Lucy practiced her dance routine for 48 minutes. She stopped practicing at 6:03 p.m. What time did she start practicing?

    A. 5:25 p.m.

    B. 6:51 p.m.

    C. 5:12 p.m.

    D. 5:15 p.m.

25. Craig arrived at the library at 3:25 p.m. He left at 4:05 p.m. How many minutes was Craig at the library?

    A. 35 minutes

    B. 40 minutes

    C. 30 minutes

    D. 45 minutes

26. Melanie has a water tank with a capacity of 30 gallons. She uses a 2-quart bowl to fill the tank. How many bowls of water does she use?

    A. 15

    B. 30

    C. 60

    D. 80

27. A pool had 40 liters of water in it. After it rained overnight, there were 45 liters of water in it. How many milliliters of water were added to the pool?

    A. 5

    B. 50

    C. 500

    D. 5,000

Nancy records her monthly savings for five months as shown in the following bar graph:

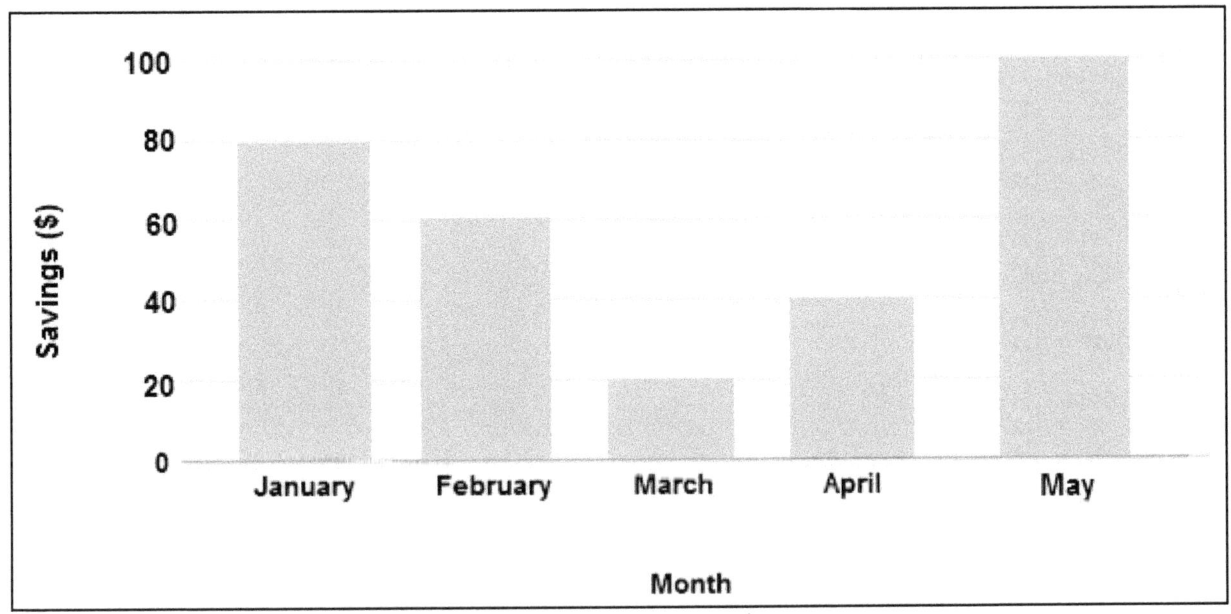

28. In which month did Nancy save the highest amount?

    A. March

    B. February

    C. January

    D. May

29. In which month did Nancy save the lowest amount?

    A. January

    B. May

    C. March

    D. February

30. How much did Nancy save in February?

    A. $80

    B. $60

    C. $20

    D. $40

31. How much more did she save in May than in March?

   A. $100

   B. $60

   C. $80

   D. $120

32. What was her total savings from January till April?

   A. $300

   B. $100

   C. $200

   D. $160

33. In June, Nancy saved $55 more than in April. How much did she save in June?

   A. $90

   B. $95

   C. $85

   D. $105

ANSWER KEY:

1) B
2) D
3) A
4) A
5) C
6) D
7) B
8) A
9) D
10) C
11) D
12) D
13) C
14) D
15) A
16) B
17) B
18) C
19) A
20) D
21) A
22) B
23) D
24) D
25) B
26) C
27) D
28) D
29) C
30) B
31) C
32) C
33) B

REFLECTION ON LEARNING

After completing Practice Test #2, reflect on your performance by answering the questions below. Discuss your responses with your instructor or a classmate.

1- What questions did you answer incorrectly? List the question numbers.

2- Review the list. What types of questions (operations, measurements, algebra, geometry, data analysis, statistics, graph, pie chart) did you answer incorrectly?

3- Review each question you've missed. Why do you think you answered the question incorrectly?

4- Based on the questions you missed, what math functions or concepts do you need to study and practice more? List them.

5- Review the question you got correctly. What strategies or methods did you use? What did you do well?

6- After reviewing all the questions, what questions do you have for your instructor?

PRACTICE TEST # 3

You have 50 minutes to answer 33 questions.

1. What is the value of the underlined digit?

   8<u>**4**</u>,763

   A. Four

   B. Four thousand

   C. Four hundred

   D. Forty thousand

2. What is the value of A?

   $$15{,}472 = A + 5{,}000 + 400 + 70 + 2$$

   A. 100

   B. 1,000

   C. 10,000

   D. 100,000

3. What is the value of the underlined digit?

   <u>**2**</u>3,871

   A. Twenty thousand

   B. Two thousand

   C. Two hundred

   D. Twenty hundred

4. A four-digit number has a 9 in the hundreds place, 4 in the tens place, 7 in the thousands place, and 5 in the ones place. What is the number?

   A. 9,475

   B. 4,975

   C. 7,495

   D. 7,945

5. Caitlin can buy 12 bars of soap for $48. How much does one cost?

   A. $5

   B. $4

   C. $3

   D. $9

6. Rick walks 2 miles every day. How many miles does he walk in 5 weeks?

   A. 35 miles

   B. 50 miles

   C. 70 miles

   D. 10 miles

Look at the following receipt:

BARBECUE

454 Avenue
New York, NY
Store#100 (212) 654-7889

2	Regular Cheese Slice	$22.00
1	Sicilian Cheese Slice	$3.00
1	20oz Bottle	$2.00

SUBTOTAL: $27.00
TOTAL ?
VISA
PURCHASE $27.00
VISA 2323
Auth#424104 Exp Date **/**
Lane #180 Cashier 986
9/13/2018 11:29 AM Ref/Seq#57367

7. How many items were purchased?

   A. 4

   B. 3

   C. 2

   D. 5

8. What is the subtotal amount?

   A. $22

   B. $3

   C. $30

   D. $27

9. What is the total amount?

   A. $27

   B. $25

   C. $22

   D. $30

10. Which item is most expensive?

   A. Sicilian cheese slice

   B. Regular cheese slice

   C. 20 oz. bottle

11. What is the cost of a dozen Sicilian cheese slice?

   A. $18

   B. $36

   C. $24

   D. $32

12. What is N?

$$5(8 + 7) = 40 + N$$

A. 12

B. 30

C. 35

D. 45

13. What is X + Y?

$$7 + 8 + 22 = X + 7 + Y$$

A. 30

B. 22

C. 14

D. 15

14. What is the unknown number?

$$? \times 4 = 44$$

A. 40

B. 11

C. 48

D. 12

15. What is the unknown number?

$$4 + 8 + ? = 24$$

A. 16

B. 18

C. 15

D. 12

16. What is the circumference of a circle with a diameter of 100 inches? (Use $\pi = 3.14$)

    A. 314 in.

    B. 31.4 in.

    C. 157 in.

    D. 3,140 in.

17. If the radius of a circle is 8 centimeters, what is the area? (Use $\pi = 3.14$)

    A. 50.24 cm^2

    B. 100.48 cm^2

    C. 200.96 cm^2

    D. 25.12 cm^2

Look at the following rectangle

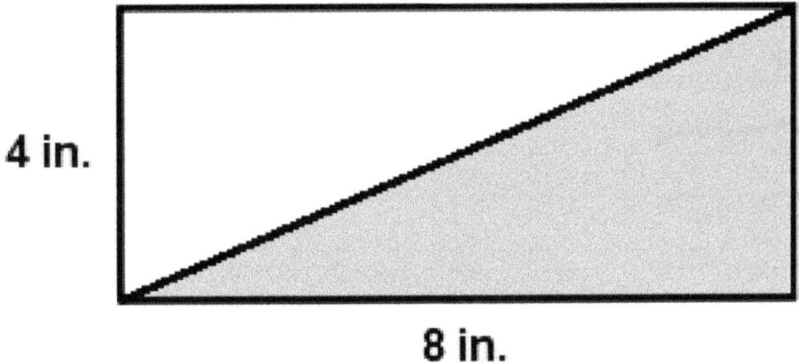

18. What is the perimeter of the rectangle?

    A. 12 in.

    B. 32 in.

    C. 20 in.

    D. 24 in.

19. What is the area of the rectangle?

    A. 32 in^2

    B. 16 in^2

    C. 24 in^2

    D. 36 in^2

20. What is the area of the shaded triangle?

A. 12 in^2

B. 28 in^2

C. 16 in^2

D. 15 in^2

21. What is the missing value?

10 meters = ? centimeters

A. 100

B. 1,000

C. 10

D. 1

Look at the following drawing:

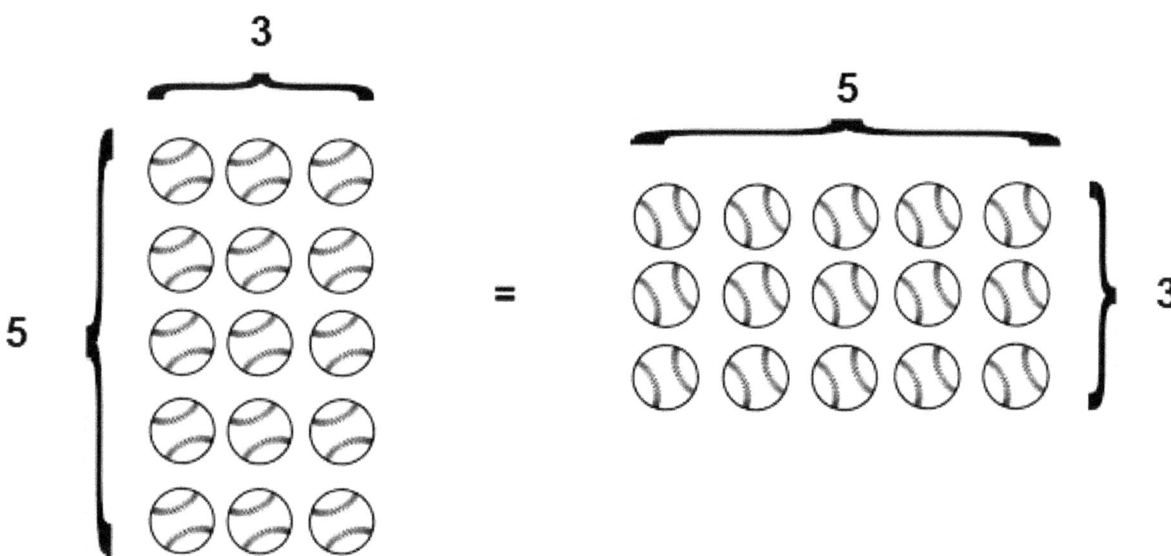

22. Which expression represents the drawing?

A. 3 + 5 = 5 + 3

B. 3 x 5 = 5 x 3

C. 3 x 5 = 5 + 3

D. 3(4 +1) = 5 + 3

23. Which property represents the drawing?

    A. Commutative Property of Addition

    B. Associative Property of Addition

    C. Commutative Property of Multiplication

    D. Distributive Property of Multiplication

24. Brooke claims that there are x hours in two weeks. What is x?

    A. 336

    B. 168

    C. 360

    D. 154

25. An airplane departs at 4:00 p.m. and arrives at 7:30 p.m. How many minutes were the passengers on the airplane for?

    A. 180 minutes

    B. 240 minutes

    C. 150 minutes

    D. 210 minutes

The following table shows the amount of food that four dogs ate in a week:

Name	**Amount of food**
Scrappy	7 kilograms
Codi	8, 500 grams
Comet	10 kilograms
Tango	12, 500 grams

26. How many kilograms did Codi eat?

    A. 85 kg.

    B. 8.5 kg.

    C. 850 kg.

    D. 8, 500 kg.

27. How many kilograms did Tango eat?

    A. 125 kg.

    B. 1.25 kg.

    C. 1, 250 kg.

    D. 12.5 kg.

28. Who ate the most?

    A. Comet

    B. Scrappy

    C. Tango

    D. Codi

Mr. Johnson surveyed some students to find out their favorite foods. The results are shown in the following bar graph:

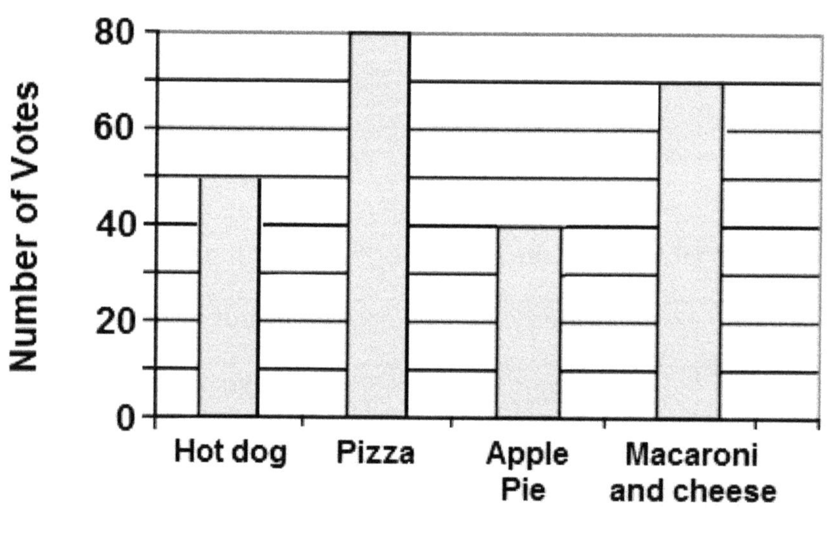

29. Which is the most popular food?

    A. Macaroni and cheese

    B. Pizza

    C. Apple pie

    D. Hot dog

30. Which is the least popular food?

    A. Pizza

    B. Apple pie

    C. Hot dog

    D. Macaroni and cheese

31. How many students said that pizza is their favorite food?

    A. 80

    B. 60

    C. 50

    D. 70

32. How many students said that the hot dog is their favorite food?

    A. 40

    B. 60

    C. 50

    D. 55

33. How many students were surveyed?

    A. 170

    B. 230

    C. 210

    D. 240

ANSWER KEY:

1) B
2) C
3) A
4) D
5) B
6) C
7) A
8) D
9) A
10) B
11) B
12) C
13) A
14) B
15) D
16) A
17) C
18) D
19) A
20) C
21) B
22) B
23) C
24) A
25) D
26) B
27) D
28) C
29) B
30) B
31) A
32) C
33) D

REFLECTION ON LEARNING

After completing Practice Test #3, reflect on your performance by answering the questions below. Discuss your responses with your instructor or a classmate.

1- What questions did you answer incorrectly? List the question numbers.

2- Review the list. What types of questions (operations, measurements, algebra, geometry, data analysis, statistics, graph, pie chart) did you answer incorrectly?

3- Review each question you've missed. Why do you think you answered the question incorrectly?

4- Based on the questions you missed, what math functions or concepts do you need to study and practice more? List them.

5- Review the question you got correctly. What strategies or methods did you use? What did you do well?

6- After reviewing all the questions, what questions do you have for your instructor?

PRACTICE TEST # 4

You have 50 minutes to answer 33 questions.

1. What is the value of the underlined digit?

   12,**5**38

   A. 5 thousand

   B. 5 tens

   C. 5 hundred

   D. 5 ones

2. What is the value of N?

   $$123{,}565 = 100{,}000 + 20{,}000 + N + 500 + 60 + 5$$

   A. 300

   B. 30,000

   C. 30

   D. 3,000

3. What is the value of the underlined digit?

   103,728

   A. One thousand

   B. One hundred thousand

   C. One ten thousand

   D. Ten hundred

4. A four-digit number has a 0 in the hundreds place, an 8 in the tens place, a 1 in the thousands place, and 6 in the ones place. What is the number?

   A. 1,086

   B. 1,806

   C. 8,106

   D. 6,801

5. A truck weighs 12,486 pounds. What is the correct way to write this number?

   A. Twelve hundred four thousand eighty-six

   B. One hundred twenty thousand four hundred eighty-six

   C. Twelve thousand four hundred eighty-six

   D. Two thousand four hundred eighty-six

Look at the following math puzzle:

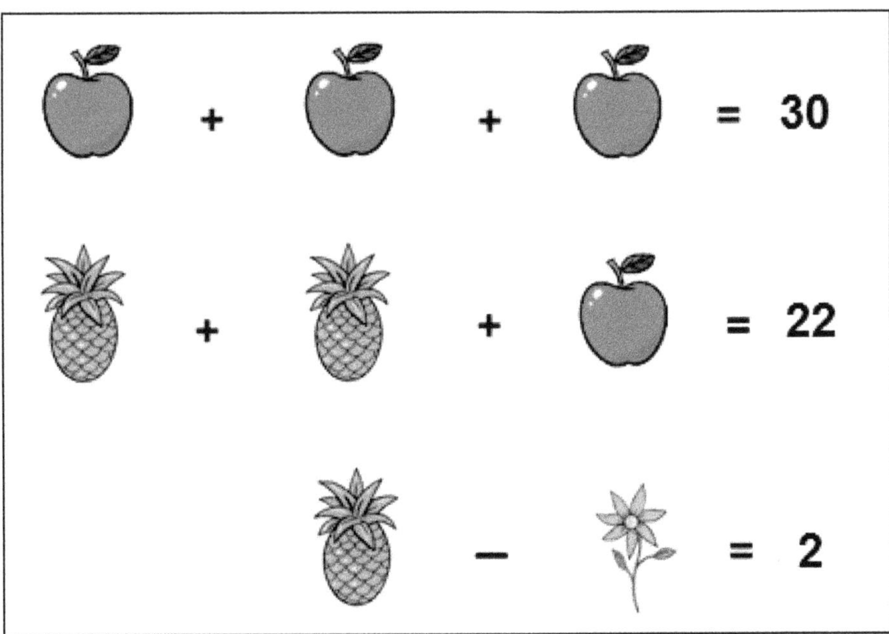

6. What is the value of an apple?

   A. 27

   B. 15

   C. 10

   D. 5

7. What is the value of a pineapple?

   A. 6

   B. 12

   C. 8

   D. 5

8. What is the value of the flower?

   A. 3

   B. 4

   C. 2

   D. 1

9. What is the value of a dozen flowers?

   A. 12

   B. 36

   C. 24

   D. 48

10. What is the value of two apples and two pineapples?

    A. 16

    B. 40

    C. 32

    D. 45

11. Two items cost $74. If one costs $28, how much did the other item cost?

    A. $46

    B. $102

    C. $56

    D. $62

Look at the following receipt:

Clover Club
210 Smith St
Brooklyn, NY 11201
718-855-7939

Server: FRONT BAR	05/11/2009
Todd/1	12:26 AM
Guests: 2	10047
Mac & Cheese Veg	11.00
Golden Girl	?
Mint Julep	11.00
Complete Subtotal	33.00
Subtotal	33.00
Tax	2.76
Total	35.76
Balance Due	**35.76**

12. How many items were purchased?

    A. 3

    B. 4

    C. 2

    D. 5

13. What is the subtotal amount?

    A. $35.76

    B. $11

    C. $33

    D. $22

14. What is the cost of a golden girl?

    A. $12

    B. $15

    C. $10

    D. $11

15. Which item is most expensive?

    A. Golden girl

    B. Mac & cheese

    C. Mint Julep

    D. None of the above

16. What is the cost of eight Mint Juleps?

    A. $18

    B. $88

    C. $98

    D. $80

17. What is Y?

$$6\,(9 + 8) = 54 + Y$$

    A. 48

    B. 14

    C. 42

    D. 16

18. What is C + D?

$$26 + 18 + 21 = C + 26 + D$$

    A. 18

    B. 21

    C. 37

    D. 39

19. What is the unknown number?

$$70 \div ? = 14$$

A. 56

B. 5

C. 12

D. 8

20. What is the unknown number?

$$(15 + 12) - ? = 18$$

A. 10

B. 9

C. 7

D. 13

21. The side lengths of a triangle are 12 in., X in., and 8 in. If the perimeter of the triangle is 32 inches, what is X?

A. 15 in.

B. 19 in.

C. 12 in.

D. 9 in.

22. If the diameter of a circle is 2 feet, what is the area? (Use $\pi = 3.14$)

A. 12.56 ft^2

B. 3.14 ft^2

C. 5.14 ft^2

D. 6.28 ft^2

Look at the following square:

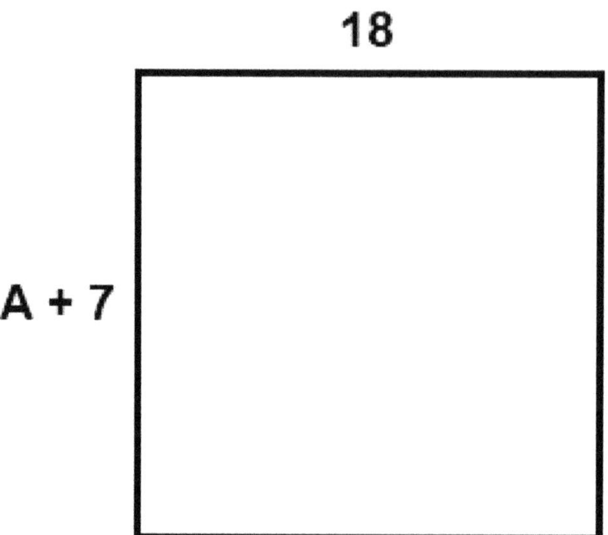

23. What is A?

    A. 8

    B. 25

    C. 13

    D. 11

24. What is the perimeter of the square?

    A. 72

    B. 36

    C. 28

    D. 82

25. What is the area of the square?

    A. 49

    B. 121

    C. 324

    D. 434

26. What is the missing value?

8 meters = ? millimeters

A. 8,000

B. 800

C. 80

D. 8

27. Patrick claims that there are M months in six years. What is M?

A. 36

B. 72

C. 78

D. 85

28. Which of the following is a non-standard unit of volume?

A. Fluid ounce

B. Gallon

C. Barrel

D. Paper clips

29. Grover worked for 5 hours and 20 minutes. How many minutes did he work?

A. 160 minutes

B. 320 minutes

C. 300 minutes

D. 290 minutes

Consider the following linear graph:

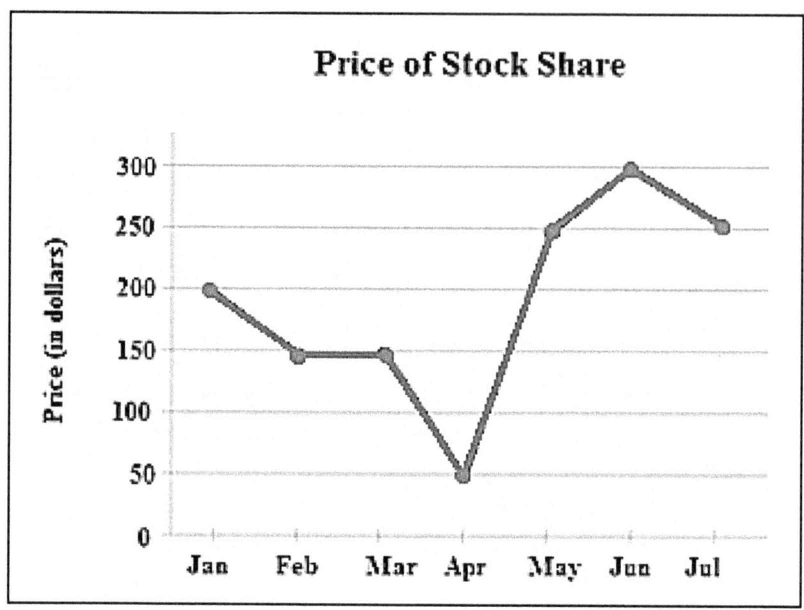

30. Which month was the greatest price registered?

    A. January

    B. May

    C. June

    D. March

31. Which month was the lowest price registered?

    A. April

    B. July

    C. February

    D. March

32. What was the price of the stock share in March?

    A. $50

    B. $100

    C. $200

    D. $150

33. What was the price of the stock share in July?

A. $300

B. $250

C. $200

D. $350

ANSWER KEY:

1) C
2) D
3) B
4) A
5) C
6) C
7) A
8) B
9) D
10) C
11) A
12) A
13) C
14) D
15) D
16) B
17) A
18) D
19) B
20) B
21) C
22) B
23) D
24) A
25) C
26) A
27) B
28) D
29) B
30) C
31) A
32) D
33) B

REFLECTION ON LEARNING

After completing Practice Test #4, reflect on your performance by answering the questions below. Discuss your responses with your instructor or a classmate.

1- What questions did you answer incorrectly? List the question numbers.

2- Review the list. What types of questions (operations, measurements, algebra, geometry, data analysis, statistics, graph, pie chart) did you answer incorrectly?

3- Review each question you've missed. Why do you think you answered the question incorrectly?

4- Based on the questions you missed, what math functions or concepts do you need to study and practice more? List them.

5- Review the question you got correctly. What strategies or methods did you use? What did you do well?

6- After reviewing all the questions, what questions do you have for your instructor?

MORE TEXTBOOKS BY CBL

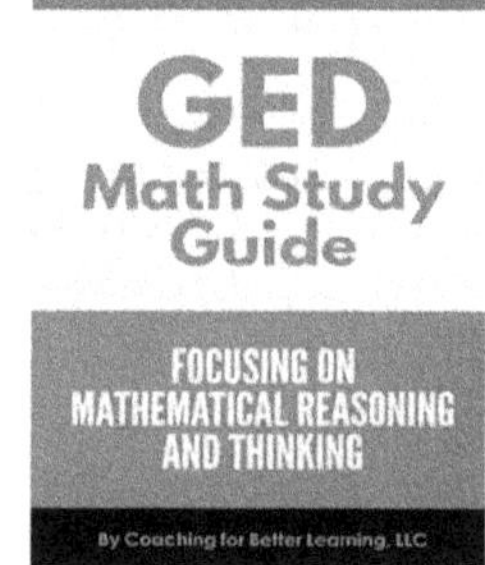

ADULT ED
MATH
NUMBER SYSTEM, NUMBER SENSE, AND OPERATIONS PREPARING
FOR
CASAS, TABE 11 & 12, HISET, AND GED TESTING
BY COACHING FOR BETTER LEARNING

ADULT ED
MATH
GEOMETRY PREPARING
FOR
CASAS, TABE 11 & 12, HISET, AND GED TESTING
BY COACHING FOR BETTER LEARNING

CBL COACHING
Math
Practice Worksheets and Workbook for Adult Students

SKILLS FOR SUCCESS IN CAREER AND TECHNICAL EDUCATION (CTE)
STUDENT GUIDE
CBL COACHING

HOW TO ACHIEVE BETTER STUDENT RETENTION IN ADULT EDUCATION
TEDDY EDOUARD

TABE 11 & 12
CONSUMABLE
STUDENT READING
MANUAL
FOR LEVEL E
By Coaching for Better Learning, LLC

TABE 11 & 12
CONSUMABLE
STUDENT READING
MANUAL
FOR LEVEL M
By Coaching for Better Learning, LLC

TABE 11 & 12
CONSUMABLE
STUDENT READING
MANUAL
FOR LEVEL D
By Coaching for Better Learning, LLC

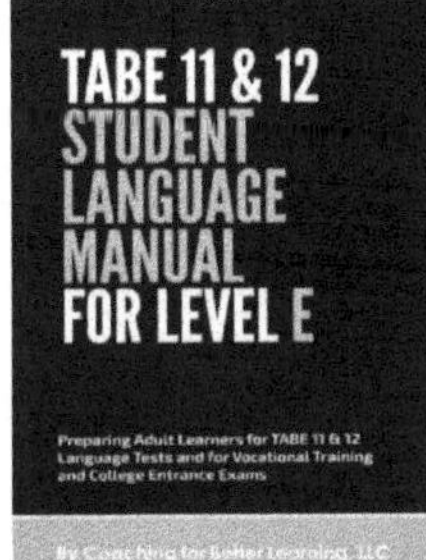
TABE 11 & 12
STUDENT
LANGUAGE
MANUAL
FOR LEVEL E

TABE 11 & 12
STUDENT
LANGUAGE
MANUAL
FOR LEVEL M
By Coaching for Better Learning, LLC

TABE 11 & 12
Consumable
Student Math
Workbook
FOR LEVEL E

TABE 11 & 12
Consumable
Student Math
Workbook
FOR LEVEL M

TABE 11 & 12
Consumable
Student Math
Workbook
FOR LEVEL D

TABE 11 & 12
Consumable
Student Math
Workbook
FOR LEVEL A

CBL COACHING
Workbook
Number and Letter Tracing for Adult Students

READING NOTEBOOK & JOURNAL
For Adult Students
By Coaching For Better Learning

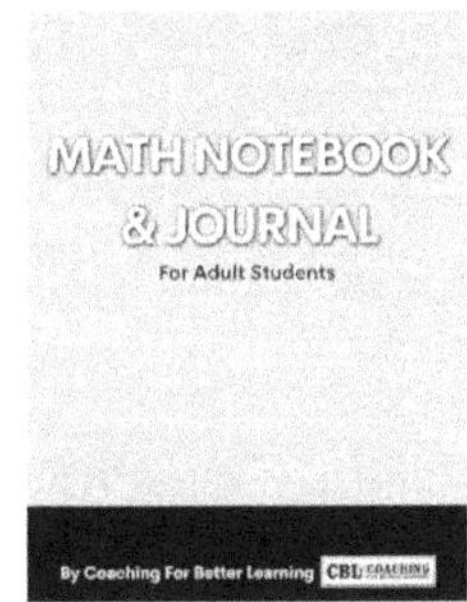
MATH NOTEBOOK & JOURNAL
For Adult Students
By Coaching For Better Learning

BOOK 1
PHONICS AND LIFE SKILLS READING
FOR
Adult Literacy, ABE, and ESL Students
CBL COACHING

BOOK 2
PHONICS AND LIFE SKILLS READING
FOR
Adult Literacy, ABE, and ESL Students
CBL COACHING

BOOK 3
PHONICS AND LIFE SKILLS READING
FOR
Adult Literacy, ABE, and ESL Students
CBL COACHING

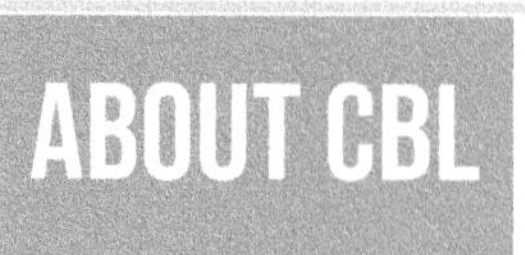

CBL equips programs and instructors to increase student retention, learning—and success.

We do it by offering evidence-based systematic solutions, learner-centered teaching materials, instructor-centered training, and future-oriented strategies in adult education, workforce development, and vocational training.

We teach proven insights, knowledge, and skills that are useful to practitioners (instructors, administrators, and support staff).

CBL also takes pride in publishing student-centered textbooks designed to prepare learners for CASAS, TABE 11&12, HiSET, and GED assessments and assist instructors in covering course curricula and standards with confidence.

Our publications also include teaching guides, test prep tools, and study guides that foster reflective learning, ensuring sustained engagement in active learning. Find our meticulously crafted textbooks on our book page (cbledu.com) or major platforms like Amazon, Barnes & Noble, and Ingram Spark.

CBL also guides adult education and workforce programs in establishing robust professional development programs—training, peer-mentoring, coaching, community of practices (CoPs), and instructional systems— fostering a culture of continuous improvement and contributing to higher learner retention and success rates. We also offer workshops and PD sessions for adult educators and classroom instructors.

If you have suggestions or questions about instructional systems, textbooks, or student learning and retention, contact us today at teamcbl@cbledu.com or 410-960-4082.

www.ingramcontent.com/pod-product-compliance
Ingram Content Group UK Ltd.
Pitfield, Milton Keynes, MK11 3LW, UK
UKHW061705190726
13853UKWH00008B/2421